Vipassana
The way to an awakened life

By
Michael Kewley
Dhammachariya Paññadipa

Copyright©Michael Kewley 2013
ISBN: 978-1-899417-12-4

Reprinted from Opening the Spiritual Heart 1996
ISBN 1-899417-04-04
Out of print

Published by:
Panna Dipa Books.

e-mail:
dhammateacher@hotmail.com

Dedication

To my late teacher and greatest inspiration in my life, Sayadaw Rewata Dhamma.

'The gift of Dhamma excels all gifts.'

Vipassana
The way to an awakened life

Originally called Opening the Spiritual Heart, this book began as a series of Vipassana retreat and course notes in Budh Gaya, India in 1991. Having just finished sitting ten day intensive meditation retreats, students began asking me to provide them with something that would not only remind than of our time together, but also support them in their daily life. I began writing the outline of the simple practices I had shared with them. These few pages were then sewn together in the town, and sold for one rupee to cover our costs.

Since that time in India, Opening the Spiritual Heart has evolved into this present book form but the reason for producing it has always remained the same: that is, to share the Dhamma and to help people find love and peace in their ordinary everyday lives. It is not necessary to go to India to discover the reasons for your unhappiness; this can be done easily in your own home. What is necessary is commitment to the reality of awakening so that we are no longer victims to the difficulties that this life occasionally offers.

I wish only the best for you and success with this course.

May all beings be happy.

Michael Kewley

Vipassana

Contents

Vipassana

Before we begin

Welcome to this structured and guided course of Vipassana (Insight) and Metta Bhavana (Loving Kindness) meditation. This programme has been designed especially for people to practice in their own home and success is assured for everyone who quietly commits in the right way.

Please follow the week by week instructions and make the effort to sit in meditation every day. The benefits that you will receive relate directly to the effort that you apply. Don't be greedy, don't be impatient, but practice with gentle and consistent effort. In this way everything will go well.

At the back of his book is a section of questions and answers. Please turn to these any time after the first week of practice. These are real questions and have been asked many times on the courses and retreats that I present. I include them and the answers to assist you in your understanding of the life enhancing practice of Vipassana and Metta Bhavana.

As well as the meditation practices outlined and explained, there is a wider view of how we already live in the world. Please read this carefully and reflect upon my words. It is not my purpose to convince you that what I say is true.

The opportunity in cultivating the practices presented here is to see and know for ourselves the nature of our mind. This then determines our attitude to life. Belief and blind faith are not part of this process.

Please apply yourself with quiet determination and just see what unfolds.

Maybe you will be amazed at how complicated you have made your life and how simple it can be.

Glossary of key terms.

Vipassana. Insight meditation, designed to develop awareness in everyday life.

Metta. The development of unconditional acceptance to the realities of life.

Bhavana. To cultivate the mind.

Let go. To release our attachment to conditions of the mind that lead to unhappiness.

Mind. The environment into which all mental states arise.

Love. Unconditional acceptance of all beings.

Compassion. The recognition that all suffering begins with mind.

Joy. The natural state of the mind that does not grasp.

Balance. Living in harmony with life itself.

Visudhimagga. The way of releasing ourselves from unwholesome thoughts.

Loving Awareness. The conclusion of our practice.

Dhamma. Buddhist word for Truth or reality.

Preliminary instructions

Vipassana Bhavana (Insight meditation) and Metta Bhavana (Loving Kindness meditation) is a very powerful practice and with it we can change everything about our life. However, we must understand that the effects experienced are in direct relationship to the effort applied. It is as though we wish to start a fire by rubbing two pieces of wood together. If we rub furiously for two minutes, rest for five minutes and then rub again for another minute we will soon become discouraged as the wood never shows the slightest sign of igniting. However, if we rub the two pieces of wood together with a consistent and determined effort, soon we will be able to enjoy the benefits of a beautiful flame. The heat and light from this flame will not only be of benefit to ourselves but, ultimately, all beings. But before we can begin the first part of the practice, we should look at the preliminary instructions.

Determination

It is necessary for you to be determined in your approach to this course and to follow the instructions to the best of your ability. It must be stressed that you should learn each aspect of practice properly, in order to fully benefit from it. This course has been designed to progress week by week; therefore, each section must be understood and practised before moving on to the next. There may be many times during the course when you feel there is just not enough time to meditate, or there is something else you would rather do, but here I ask you to remember what you are hoping to achieve and to be resolute in your undertaking.

Do not try to find the time to meditate; rather, make the time. This practice must take priority over other less important events in our life such as watching television, reading the newspaper or being distracted with your smart phone. Once or even twice a day, for the next four weeks and longer, make the time to meditate. At the end of the course, reflect upon the changes in your life and any new understanding that may have arisen. If you feel then that you no longer want to continue with the practice, you can of course let go, but you will have at least given yourself the opportunity to experience it fully.

Many people have a limited meditation experience, and perhaps you will feel inclined to add something extra to the practices that you are learning. Here I ask you to resist. The practices that you will learn during this course all work very well and have been tried and tested by hundreds of thousands of people since the time of the Buddha himself. None of them need enhancing by the addition of visualisation or mantras.

Please only follow the instructions as they are given.

Posture

In Vipassana practice, posture is not considered to be as important as in some other forms of meditation. The purpose of this meditation is the development of insight and complete understanding of the nature of our own reality, not merely the ability to sit for hour upon hour in the same posture. However, we should try to develop a posture that we can maintain for the prescribed period, and then not change it until absolutely necessary.

At the beginning, we will sit for twenty minutes each session. You may wish to experiment with posture before we begin.

In order to sit well, the body should be balanced – that is, in a good steady posture, not leaning forward or back and with the spine reasonably straight. The hands should rest easily in the lap. The head should not fall forward and the chin should be gently tucked in, so that the slope of the nose runs straight down. This gives a good indication of balance and whether you are sitting cross-legged on the floor, kneeling on a meditation stool or simply using a straight backed chair, a good posture will help you to focus the mind and stay alert.

If the posture is too relaxed, it will encourage day dreaming and even sleep; if the posture is too rigid and tense, it will bring pain. As with all things in life, balance is everything. To find a good posture may take practice and some experimentation, but it is always a worthwhile endeavour.

As already said, for the first week of the course we will sit each time for only twenty minutes. Gradually during the course this will be increased to thirty five minutes. This may sound daunting at first, but in time it will come naturally and easily. So be patient and find the posture most suitable for your body. There is a common misconception that meditation is about sitting like the Buddha in the full lotus posture. This is absolutely not true, so find the posture that suits you and that you can maintain, initially for twenty minutes, without moving.

Location

As we begin our daily sitting practice at home, we will find that certain conditions need to be fulfilled in order to be successful. The first condition is that of a suitable location.

The location for meditation practice needs to be quiet, warm, dry, draught free and somewhere where you won't be easily disturbed. For most people, this means the bedroom, but it is for you to discover the best place in your home yourself. Try to use the same place every day and make it your special meditation place. There is no need to decorate the walls with spiritual paintings or set up a Buddhist or Christian shrine, but just keep a special area for your daily practice. Solitude, or at least privacy, is the best condition.

Sitting time

At the beginning of the course we should learn to sit well for not less than twenty minutes. This means that we should allow ourselves at least half an hour overall, taking time at the beginning to settle ourselves on our cushion or chair and time at the end to be still and quiet and to continue to experience the peaceful effects of the meditation.

It is not a good idea to try to squeeze the practice in between frantic bursts of activity such as running up the stairs at meditation time and then, twenty minutes later, rushing back downstairs to watch the news on television. We have to allow ourselves time. This practice is important, and we should have the right attitude to it.

It is also necessary to understand that whatever length of time we decide upon at the beginning of our sitting practice, we should try to our best to accomplish. No matter how badly we think our meditation sitting is going we should resolve to maintain our posture until the end and not finish until the allotted time is past. We must not allow the mind to trick us into giving up. This is very important, so at the beginning learn to sit well for twenty minutes and don't be impatient to increase the time too quickly.

These, then, are the preliminary instructions for Vipassana (Insight) and Metta Bhavana (Loving Kindness) meditation.

Vipassana

Week One.

Looking for happiness.
Living in the world.

Happiness is a goal common to all human beings. It is the very reason for everything that we do. From the moment that we awaken in the morning, to the moment we sleep again at night, it is our strongest and most persistent desire. And yet, happiness itself is so illusive. Even though it is the only thing that we want all the time, we cannot manufacture or create the feeling of it at will. We cannot make it arrive, nor can we make it stay once it has arrived. Happiness, like all other aspects of mind, is impermanent and comes and goes as it chooses, not as we decide.

Try this simple test. Tomorrow morning, when you awaken, say to yourself: 'Today I will be happy all day', and see if it is possible. As long as we don't understand this, we chase happiness like a dog chases its tail, always going around in the same small circle, acquiring, using, discarding and acquiring again.

We seek our happiness in the material world through the accumulation of possessions, hoping that each one will bring that permanent, pleasant, comfortable feeling we crave so much. The new car, smart phone, digital camera, home entertainment centre – the list is endless!

And yet, even if these possessions do bring a feeling of happiness with them, it does not and cannot last. Soon this one thing that you could not live without simply becomes something else in your already full house; another thing to insure, to worry about and repair when it breaks down. In reality, it becomes just an extra burden in our life – something else to carry.

We seek our happiness in the emotional world, wanting someone to love us and treat us in a way that we feel is appropriate. We seek the approval of others, needing their voice to tell us if we look good and are right in our own views and opinions. We feel inadequate and constantly search for the support of our friends and family or particular social, religious or cultural groups. However, if we don't get, or at least feel, supported in life, we suffer. The fundamental truth that you need to understand is that no-one, no matter who, has the power to make you happy all the time. Even if we find our perfect, life partner, daily living together bursts that particular bubble. We pin our hopes on the perfect person in the perfect relationship to make us happy all the time and they always fail us. How can it be different?

In the religious or spiritual world, we also seek our happiness. In this so called 'New Age', there are so many things that we can do: yoga, martial arts, stylized forms of meditation, re-birthing… We feel that if only we could discover who we were in a previous life we would be happy forever. Even changing our religion has the motivation of happiness behind it, yet to say that I used to believe in God, but now I believe in Allah, doesn't actually help. It is still falling into the trap of looking for happiness OUTSIDE ourselves. And this is why you are reading these words. Everything that you have tried so far in your life has failed you and your expectations. Now you feel that perhaps a course in Vipassana and Metta Bhavana will help you and, actually, it will!

Vipassana and Metta Bhavana is not about creating more ultimately impermanent feelings of happiness. This beautiful and unique form of mediation and lifestyle has the function of realising for ourselves the source of our unhappiness and then releasing it from our lives. It is not about doing just one more thing to bring happiness or even being peaceful as we sit in meditation, rather it is about recognising intuitively the conditions that we habitually empower that take us to the unpleasant feelings we call unhappiness.

As our understanding deepens we will recognise the truth of 'self responsibility': that the world we experience is the one we create for ourselves, moment after moment. With experience of the practice we will know that the feelings of happiness and unhappiness arise within us and that, in reality, no-one can make us happy and no-one can make us unhappy either. This power belongs only to us. And if it is only ourselves who can create the world that we experience, then it is only ourselves who can change that world – from stressful to calm, fearful to loving, foolish to wise.

The responsibility for the quality of your life lies only with yourself.

The material world is only what it is. It doesn't have the power to bring lasting happiness into your life, but that doesn't mean that you can't enjoy it. The emotional world, with partners, friends and family, is only what it is; it doesn't have the power to bring lasting happiness into your life, but that doesn't mean that you can't enjoy it. The spiritual world is only what it is; it doesn't have the power to bring lasting happiness into your life, but that doesn't mean that you can't enjoy it.

With true understanding, everything is seen to be what it is and so can be enjoyed if it is pleasant, or patiently endured if it is unpleasant. In this way we will live fully and freely in life, no longer looking outside ourselves, in any direction, for happiness.

Anapanasati: mindfulness of breathing

Stop a galloping horse!

Anapanasati (mindfulness of breathing) is the foundation of our whole practice. Therefore, it is extremely important to give time and effort to this simple, yet difficult, meditation practice. If we are to build a house, we cannot start with the roof. We must start with the foundations and those foundations have to be secure and strong enough to support the rest of the building.

Using the instructions below, you are encouraged to take this practice into your daily life and sit for twenty minutes each day for the first week, making mindfulness of breathing your only practice.

Many years ago in Japan there were master sword makers. These men would arise very early in the morning, purify themselves, wear their ceremonial robes, light incense and begin their work. First, heating the coals and the metal, then hammering and folding it, cooling it and repeating the process over and over until, finally, the most beautiful 'katana' (the killing sword) had been produced. Once the sword was completed it was offered to a Samurai warrior, who would be enthusiastic to test this newly acquired weapon. In those days in Japan this was not a problem and the Samurai would arrive at the local prison, where he would select three or four unfortunate prisoners, tie them together, raise his sword and with one single sweep of the blade, cut these poor people in half.[1]

It is said that Vipassana is the Samurai sword of the mind and that with it we can cut through the doubts, delusions and confusions of life, but the cutting edge of that sword is Anapanasati, mindfulness of breathing. This is the importance of this meditation practice.

For most of us the breath is not something that we are usually aware of, unless we have been involved in a physical activity or have some kind of respiratory complaint. However, whether we are aware of it or not, the body inhales and exhales all day, every day. So, here is the profound truth that you need to reflect upon: you don't breathe – the body breathes! Whether we are awake or asleep, conscious or unconscious, the body breathes, naturally and by itself.

Beginning

So, how to begin? Once we have assumed our posture and feel comfortable and at ease, we can allow our eyes to gently close and let the breath naturally, without forcing the last cubic centimetre from our lungs, leave the body.

---

1   I do not know if any part of this story is true. It was told to me by my teacher to illustrate the value of giving time and effort to the practice of Anapanasati.

Because the breath is a very subtle object to notice, we need at first to be very precise with our attention to it and so, as the natural inhalation begins, we mentally note that point with the word IN. As the breath continues into the body, we again mentally note its presence with the word IN. And finally, at the point where the natural inhalation ends, we again mentally note with the word IN.

As these three stages are happening, our attention stays firmly fixed at the nostrils. We do not follow the breath into the body, nor on the exhalation do we visualise the breath leaving the body.
Once the inhalation is finished, the exhalation will begin. As one naturally conditions the other, we do not need to force ourselves to exhale; it will spontaneously arise and our attention is once again given to mentally noting the beginning, middle and end of this out-breath. This time we use the word OUT.

What could be simpler than that? To mentally note the beginning, middle and end of each inhalation and each exhalation. The purpose of this part of the practice is to refine our field of awareness from being very large and scattered, to a much smaller one – namely the movement of breath in the nostrils.

The Breath Body

As we continue to gently note the beginning, middle and end of each inhalation and each exhalation, we will soon begin to feel a sense of relaxation and peace descend upon us. This may take only one or two minutes, but it is at this point that we should let go of the noting part of the practice and be with what is known as the BREATH BODY. This means to simply be with the breath as it enters and leaves the nose. This is the second aspect of Anapanasati (mindfulness of breathing).

Now we are with the breath from its very beginning through the middle until the end, simply being aware. We do not try to change to or alter it in any way, but allow the body to breathe at its own natural rhythm. We no longer break the breath down into separate parts, but experience it now as a whole process without interruption.

It is during this part of our practice that we will quite spontaneously begin to notice the main object for awareness, simply called the TOUCH SENSATION OF BREATH. Each time we inhale and exhale, whether we are aware of it or not, a sensation arises in the nostrils. It is important to understand that you do not create this sensation and that you are not making it happen; also, that this sensation is not special, magical, mystical or, worse, 'spiritual'. It is simply the natural sensation that arises when the breath contacts the sensitive parts of the nostrils as we breathe. As our awareness grows stronger we notice this impersonal sensation more and more clearly, that is all.

Each one of us may experience this sensation in different ways and in different places in the nose. Perhaps you will feel it at the tip of the nose, or in the middle or higher up, or the location will change with the in-breath and the out-breath, but wherever you feel a sensation in the nose connected to the breath, that's it!

Often I am asked: "What will the touch sensation of breath feel like?" For this I cannot say and you will have to discover the specific quality for yourself. Perhaps it will be a coolness as the breath enters the nostrils, or a warmth as the breath leaves. Perhaps it will be an indefinable sensation with no particular quality, but whatever sensation arises in the nostrils connected to the natural breath, that's it!

As always in a mature spiritual practice, the advice is the same: don't look for something special! When we look for something special, we miss what is happening right now in this moment.

At one time there was a man who lived in a town that was ravaged by a large flood. The water rose higher and higher and so the man found himself sitting on the roof of his house. A rescue boat arrived and the men in the boat said: "Come on, get into the boat and we will save you."
"No" said the man, "it's okay, I put my trust in God.

He'll save me." And so the men rowed away.
The water continued to rise and soon it was up to the man's chest. Another rescue boat arrived and the men said: "Come on, get into the boat and we will save you."
"No" said the man, "it's okay, I put my trust in God. He'll save me." And so the men rowed away.
The water continued to rise and soon it was up to the man's chin. This time, a helicopter hovered overhead and lowered a rope. The pilot shouted: "Quick, take the rope and we will save you."
"No" said the man, "it's okay, I put my trust in God. He'll save me." And so the helicopter flew away. The water continued to rise and soon the man drowned. He arrived in heaven, feeling quite angry. He marched straight up to God and said: "I have believed in you, all my life. I thought you would have saved me!" "Well" said God, "I really don't know what happened. I sent two boats and a helicopter."

Once there is awareness of the touch sensation of breath, that immediately becomes the meditation object and we simply stay with that until the meditation session is finished. Cultivating the awareness necessary to notice the touch sensation of breath may not happen in the first few sittings of practice, but with gentle and consistent effort it will arrive. Be patient and simply sit, as instructed.

So, now we have the touch sensation of breath, experienced as the focal point of our meditation. Once mindfulness of this has been well established we should let our attention rest upon it, simply being aware as this sensation arises and passes away. Each time there is an inhalation the sensation arises. Each time there is an exhalation the sensation arises. The sensation arises with the act of breathing and is not separate from it.

In the same way as when we use a saw to cut a piece of wood, our attention is fixed at the point where the teeth actually cut the wood, rather than following our arm backwards and forwards. During the practice of Anapanasati, our attention must rest at the point where the sensation arises in the nostrils and not follow the breath in and out of the body.

We can also use the example of a large stone on the beach to help us understand this. When the waves roll up the beach they wash all around the stone, touching it on all sides, but the stone itself does not move up the beach with them. The stone stays firmly where it is. Equally, when the waves roll back down the beach they touch the stone on all sides, but again the stone does not move with them. The stone experiences the water, whilst not being overwhelmed by it.

This must be our attitude with regard to the touch sensation of breath: to let the concept of breathing fall away and simply be with the sensation of breath as it arises and passes with each inhalation and each exhalation.

This, then, is the practice of Anapanasati, also called mindfulness of breathing. It is a powerful form of meditation and an excellent way to develop the focused mind necessary for the cultivation of awareness and love, so important in our life and for our own unconditional happiness.

Summary

Here we can review the practice. Firstly, to establish an initial level of concentration or focused mind, we turn away from the mind's usual endless activity and give our attention to the natural process of breathing. Carefully, and as precisely as possible, we mentally note the beginning, middle and end of each inhalation and each exhalation, using the words, IN, IN, IN and OUT, OUT, OUT.

Once this level of focus has been developed and we have experienced a sense of peace and calm, we can allow the noting to fall away and be with the Breath Body, the unhindered movement of air in the nostrils. Finally, during the observation of the Breath Body, the experience of the Touch Sensation of Breath will arise and this becomes the mediation object.

One final and important word before we begin our first sitting practice.
The Buddha said that: "It is easier to tame a wild animal than to train your own mind." This is exactly what you will

discover for yourself during the practice of Anapanasati. For all the years of our life we have encouraged this mind to think, plan, speculate, fantasise, remember and worry. This process will not stop just because we want to sit quietly and watch the breath. Because of this life long habit there is bound to be resistance to our meditation practice. This mind wants to be busy and stimulated. It wants to plan, it wants to remember, it wants to think. We cannot stop this from happening, but we can stop indulging it. Remember our determination.

One person told me on a course such as this that he liked to think a thought until it is finished. Sounds good, except thinking is never finished! This thought conditions the next thought and that thought conditions the one after that. The thinking process is endless and even follows us into sleep, where we call it dreaming. So be strong. The moment that you notice that your attention is not with the breath, bring it back to the touch sensation of breath. Don't get lost in thinking or fantasy or any other distraction of the mind.

The mind may try to convince you of the futility of this practice, encouraging you to give up and do something more interesting. Again, don't listen. Sit quietly and patiently and, as much as you can, keep you attention fixed on the touch sensation of breath. The moment you notice that the attention has wandered, bring it back.

Perhaps you will find that from the very moment you close your eyes your mind will wander. This is not a problem. It is certainly going to happen sooner or later, so be prepared. And don't worry, you are not doing anything wrong. This is the nature of the mind.

Perhaps you will feel that the whole twenty minutes (recommended sitting time at the beginning) has been spent recognising that the attention is not with the meditation object, so you have returned it to the breath over and over. Again, this is not a problem and there is no reason to feel discouraged. The important thing is to cultivate a loving attitude to our practice and not allow anger or frustration to creep in.

It is as though the mind is a small puppy. If we put the puppy in the middle of the floor and say "stay", what happens? The puppy runs around just as it pleases. If we return him to the centre of the room again and repeat "stay", it still has no effect. We cannot blame this little dog, because at this moment it does not know how to stay. But, patiently and lovingly, we repeat the process of returning him to the centre of the room until finally he does stay.

In all meditation training, as in life, attitude is everything. We must be gentle and kind to ourselves and not make the demand that we become experts in everything at the first attempt.

So, in the beginning we simply keep returning our attention to the object of meditation, the moment that we notice it has wandered away. If we loose our focus completely we simply start again, with IN, IN, IN. This is not a competition and it is not a fight. It is a simple yet difficult practice that we have to give our patient attention to.

Another ploy of the mind to distract us from our practice is by the way of physical sensations. To feel that the body is leaning forward or back or to the side is a common experience for people new to meditation. Resist opening your eyes to verify your posture, everything will be fine. In all my years of sharing this practice with others, no-one has ever fallen over in meditation, no matter what the mind has told them!

Tickles and itches are treated in the same way. Ignore them if possible. However, if a particular tickle or itch is really persistent and the impulse to scratch it is overwhelming, use that movement as a part of the mediation.

Keeping your eyes closed, but moving your awareness to your hand, slowly and mindfully, raise your hand to your face (if that is where the itch is) and scratch. Notice how this feels. It is not the same feeling as when you scratch without reflection or awareness. Return your hand to its former position and take your attention back to the breath.

In meditation practice it is better not to move but if you do need to change your posture, as with itch scratching, use this as an integral part of the practice. With awareness, slowly, silently and mindfully change your posture and return to the meditation object again. In this way we do not start and stop the meditation, but use everything as part of our practice.

As already mentioned, for the first week of practice the recommended time for sitting each day is twenty minutes. This may sound daunting at first, but in reality it not a huge amount of time from your day, no matter how busy you are. You only need to prioritise your intention to practice and make it more important than watching the television, for example.

At the end of your sitting time, before opening your eyes, allow the awareness to go to the body and simply experience how the body feels in this moment. Begin with your head and lightly pass the attention down through the body, taking about one minute. When you arrive at your feet, return to the breath and then open your eyes.

This, then, is the beautiful practice of Anapanasati. To simply experience the breath as sensation in the nostrils brings with it a great sense of peace and calm, so now for twenty minutes and daily for the next week we can put this simple meditation into practice.

Please establish your posture, close your eyes and turn your attention to the natural breath...

Week two

Vipassana: to see things as they really are.
*Everything that arises passes away
and is not what you are.*

This is now week two of our four part course of insight (Vipassana) and loving kindness (Metta Bhavana) meditation. Every day, for the past seven days, you have been sitting for not less than twenty minutes with the practice of Anapanasati. You have been experiencing the natural rhythm of breath, by resting your attention on the sensation that spontaneously arises with each inhalation and each exhalation.

By now you will have noticed how busy the mind really is and how quickly it becomes distracted, but each time the attention has wandered away from the breath you have returned it with loving patience. You have not indulged in thinking or fantasy, but have been disciplined and practiced, in accordance with the instructions. Now, based upon your experience with this most important style of meditation, you can begin the next part of your practice.

The word Vipassana comes from the Buddhist language of Pali and means 'to see things as they really are'. The only purpose of Vipassana practice is to see clearly the true nature of mind and body and so understand exactly where all our experiences of unhappiness and discontent really begin.

It is always our habit to blame other people and situations for the way we feel in different moments, using expressions such as "It's your fault I'm angry" or "It's because of you that I feel this way", but in reality this is our delusion. Our thoughts, moods, feelings and emotions begin and end with ourselves. No-one gives them to us and no-one can take them away. We do it to ourselves – always! Once we begin to understand the implications of this realisation fully, we are in a position to change everything about our life.

There was once a Samurai who began to reflect upon his life. He had been in battle many times and killed many men. In one moment of awareness he began to wonder about the outcome of such a violent life. When he died would he go to heaven or hell? This question troubled him for many days until he realised that he needed the assistance of a Zen master to help him with this difficulty.

The Samurai went to a nearby monastery and approached the master.

"Excuse me," he said, "but I need to ask you a question. Is there a heaven and a hell?"

The master looked unkindly at the Samurai and replied somewhat rudely: "And just who are you?"

"I am a Samurai", he answered proudly.

"You, a Samurai?", said the master. "I don't believe it. Just look at you. Your clothes are dirty and torn, your

top knot has fallen to one side, and I doubt that the sword you carry could even cut through butter."
The Samurai was instantly furious to be spoken to in such a disrespectful way and drew his sword to cut down the master. After all, to kill one more man would really mean nothing now. Just as the sword was at its highest point, the master, with only love in his eyes, looked at the Samurai and said: "Here open the gates of hell."
The Samurai was intelligent and knew that he had received a teaching. Now humbly returning his sword to its scabbard he bowed low.
"And here opens the gates of heaven," continued the master.

Heaven and hell. This is the choice for all of us. Which world do you want to live in, because it is you who is creating the conditions of the world that you meet in every moment.

We live in a society and culture where emotion, passion and strong feelings are held in high regard. To have these qualities means to be alive, to live life to the full. In fact, someone without passion and emotion may be called a 'cold fish'. This is the usual state of affairs and is how life is presented for so called 'normal people'. We find our lives bound to an endless round of mood swings, thoughts, feelings and emotions, without ever examining where they really come from and what kind of difficulties they can lead us into.

By not understanding the nature of the mind, we will

always find ourselves victim to it – at the mercy of whatever manifests, always far, far away from the balanced mind that is peaceful and in harmony with life itself.

Often we can hear the English expression 'to be a victim of circumstance', meaning that we are under the influence of external conditions, without any free will to make choices or changes. However, the reality is that we are never a victim of the external world; we are only ever a victim to our own mind and the endless series of mind states that it presents.

Each morning, upon awakening, we experience a mental state. Depending upon conditions, this mental state can be happy or sad, angry or peaceful, or filled with desire or regret. The mind can manifest in any way whatsoever, but it is with this initial mind state that we begin our day. Without realising it, we become overwhelmed by the mind and so take on the qualities of it. If anger is present, we simply become angry. If fear is present, we simply become afraid. If depression is present, we simply become depressed. Whatever mind state arises we embrace completely and become that thing. There is no separation between what we experience and our relationship to it.

It is as though our mind is a clear pool of water. This we can say is its natural state. Into this pool are dropped many different coloured dyes, each one representing a different thought, mood, feeling or emotion and each one turning the water completely to its own hue. The mind itself may not know the colour it has become or where the dye that tainted it came from, but the effects of changing colour so many times a day is readily experienced. This experience we define as unhappiness, demonstrating our unsatisfactory relationship not only to the mind, but to life itself. It is exactly the recognition of this experience that has brought you to the practice of meditation: that is, the inability to control the mind and so always fall victim to it.

As long as the mind and our lack of understanding into its real nature remains unchallenged, we will never experience true peace in our lives and so will always be victim to that which we ultimately cannot control.

If it were truly possible to control the mind, each one of us without exception, upon awakening in the morning, would say: 'Today I will be happy all day'. Tomorrow morning when you wake, say it to yourself and see if you can be. If happiness could be determined simply by an act of will, the world and our personal experience of it would be a very different place.

The reality is not like that. It is as though we are a piece of cork floating on the ocean.
When good fortune comes our way we are lifted high and ride the crest of the wave, enjoying all the pleasant mental states that we label 'happiness'. However, when misfortune arrives we sink down, low into the trough of the wave, suffering the unpleasant mental states that we

label 'unhappiness'.

This is how life is for everyone who has never examined the relationship of self to the mind. Whether we consider ourselves intelligent or not is not the issue here. Intelligence is not wisdom, and it is only wisdom – the clear seeing and comprehension of reality – that will transform us from being the helpless victim to the mind that we experience.

This mind is not yours! You don't own it and you don't control it. This mind never asks your permission to appear and dominate your life. It never says, 'Excuse me, do you mind if I become jealous now?' or 'Is it alright if I am stressed now, or anxious, or fearful etc...?' So, how can we live in harmony with this invisible power that dominates our life, so that our life experience is one of joy, balance and love?

Through the practice of Vipassana meditation and living, we begin to recognise that a metal state is only a mental state: something that comes and goes by itself and, in every moment and in every circumstance, only ever has the power that we give it.

This mind arises and passes away, moment after moment, and it is through Vipassana practice that we can know directly this process and see the truth behind it: that each thought, mood, feeling and emotion is like a cloud passing through a clear blue empty sky. We can see it, we can know its quality, we can experience its presence in the moment, but we don't have to take a hold of it. And we hold the mind through indulgence and repression; both give each particular mind state its power.

So our way is to let go. If it is the real nature of the mind to pass away, why try to hold it anyway? If it is something pleasant, enjoy it while it is here – but don't try to hold on to it. If it is something unpleasant, relax and be with it peacefully – soon it will pass. This is the way to be with the mind and not be a victim to it; the way of letting go.

If we let go a little, there is a little peace.
If we let go a lot, there is a lot of peace.
If we let go completely: complete peace.

Complete peace, arising from a mind no longer in conflict with itself and no longer deluded by the different mind states that manifest.

From this understanding we can recognise that depression, the kind of feeling you might experience on a cold dark January morning when you have to leave your bed to go to a job that you don't particularly like, is actually only depression – a mind state that arises due to conditions. It's not you, it's not yours and it's not what you are. It is something that you can experience without becoming it. Do you understand?

The mind is not what you are, it is only that which

you become in different moments. When we are able to be with any mind state (such as anxiety) peacefully, without trying to make it go away, or, conversely, when we stop trying to hold on to pleasant mind states, the mind ceases to have any power in our life.

When we realise this, we can just be with the mind and let it be, without wishing or demanding that this moment of mind be any other way. We can know it and acknowledge it but, most importantly, be at peace with it.

Now we can experience the mental state of depression, but not be depressed; we can experience the mental state of anger, but not be angry; we can experience the mental state of fear, but not be afraid.

We can take a step back from the activity of the mind itself and experience it for what it really is: a never ending stream of thoughts, moods, feelings and emotions, arising from a beginningless beginning and moving towards an endless end. This is the nature of the mind that we call ours, take responsibility for, but have no real control over.

Our attitude here, as always, is very important. When we are aware of this endless procession of mind states, we must be with them in a friendly manner and never from a position of hostility. After all, they have all come to show us the same thing: that everything is impermanent and only has the power that we give it.

We must greet them when they arrive, but not spend time with them. They can be there, but we have no more than a passing interest. Something along the lines of: "Oh, hello anger, my old friend. I can't be with you right now because I must watch my breath. You can stay if you want to but I'm not interested at all."

It is the same, of course, for all our mental states. Through the clarity of understanding, developed through our practice of Vipassana, we can allow the mind to be exactly as it is in any moment and not be disturbed by it. Anger is only anger. Fear is only fear. Doubt is only doubt.

Here we set ourselves free from the very source of our unhappiness: that is, the mind itself. With this new found freedom, we experience life in a much more open and complete way.

The same principles are applied to the body; to recognise that heat, cold, pleasure, pain and all other physical sensations are simply phenomena arising and passing away. Of course, in different situations we must respond to the moment, but our response should come from wisdom – not just blind reaction or fear.

In the mind and body complex (that which we call 'self'), everything that arises passes way and is not what we are. This is the great liberating principle: as we begin to understand it more and more at the heart or intuitive level, we will spontaneously experience life more beautifully and peacefully, as we release the conditions of mind that only ever take us to unhappiness.

In traditional Buddhist teaching this is called the Visudhimagga – the path of purification; to let go of the conditions of our suffering or unhappiness.

And so, the origin of all our difficulties in life is not something outside ourselves. It is only our attachment and belief that the mind we experience and that which we call 'our self' are the same thing. Once we begin to wake up from this particular delusion, freedom awaits us.

You are not the mind.
This mind is not what you are.
Freedom is not something to get, it is only something to realise.

Vipassana practice (part one)
Bare Attention

As you have already understood, the meditation practice of Vipassana is firmly established upon the touch sensation of breath, as we have experienced during the week with Anapanasati. Once you are familiar with the touch sensation of breath as your meditation object, you can begin to open this practice into Vipassana meditation and be with the mind as it naturally manifests in different moments.

In the practice of Anapanasati, you were given the instruction that the breath was the most important thing and that your intention was to hold your awareness there until the end of the meditation sitting. In any moment when you noticed that the awareness had wandered away, you were to return it to the touch sensation of breath immediately. You were not to give any consideration to where the mind had wandered to, but to simply return it to the breath. It is here where the two practices separate.

Now the instruction is that before you return the awareness to the breath, once you have realised that it has wandered off, you must notice where it has wandered to. This means that if you notice thinking is taking place, instead of being with the breath, you must mentally acknowledge that this is what is happening in this moment. Having done that, you return your attention to the breath.

If you hear a sound the same conditions apply. You must notice that hearing has occurred, before returning to the breath. If you notice a fragrance in the room or a sensation in the body, simply be aware of that and return your attention to the breath.

We simply notice the natural movements of mind and we harmonise with them. Here there can be no distraction to our meditation, because whatever arises in the mind becomes our meditation object in that moment.

This practice is known as 'Bare Attention', which means to give just enough attention to a mental object as it arises, to be aware of it, but not enough to indulge or repress it. To notice each sense that is stimulated, whether seeing, tasting, touching, hearing, smelling or any movement of mind, as natural functions of the mind-body complex. Not me, not mine, not what I am. To develop the habit of choiceless awareness: not seeking only certain predetermined experiences, but being completely open and accepting of whatever the mind presents.

To sit calmly and peacefully amidst the impersonal movements of mind and body and to simply be aware of them is Vipassana meditation.

In simple words, we now give our permission for the mind to do anything it wants, of which we will be the peaceful observer.

One time in India, a young man on retreat came to

me and said: "Every time I close my eyes to meditate, I hear Beatles songs in my head. What should I do?" I replied simply: "Let it be."

Hearing the song isn't important. It's singing along that brings all the difficulties. Do you understand?

The quality of a thought isn't important either. For example, the noble thought that you would like to save all the whales in the oceans has exactly the same value as the most ignoble thought that you want to hurt or abuse someone. These are movements of mind only, conditioned by your past. They arise and pass away without your consent. You can't change them but you can be aware of them and it is that very awareness that takes away their power. Now you can respond. You can do whatever is appropriate. However, if you neither indulge nor repress these thoughts, they will fall away by themselves and you will be walking the path of Visudhimagga.

The point of practice is to notice the impersonal movements of mind and, by being aware of them, not be overwhelmed into thinking that they are realities for us. Everything we experience only ever has the power that we give it.

It is the same for all our senses. A sound is only a sound; a taste is only a taste; a touch is only a touch; a smell is only a smell and a sight is only a sight. Everything else is a personal imagination. Good or bad, right or wrong, beautiful or ugly are all perceptions of mind – part of how we live, but not realities in themselves.

To illustrate, imagine that you are sitting comfortably in a quiet room with two doors. You are peaceful and at ease, when a man walks in through one door and stands in front of you. It is enough in this moment simply to notice MAN. You don't have to notice if he's tall or short, fat or thin, young or old. Simply to notice MAN is enough and, if you don't invite this man to stay (indulgence) and you don't try to throw him out either (repression), he will leave by himself. When he leaves in this way (letting go) he will never return. This is the process of Visudhimagga.

Next into this room a woman arrives and the same conditions apply. Simply to notice WOMAN is enough. No need to go further than that to see if she is young or old, tall or short, fat or thin. WOMAN is enough, and if you don't invite her to stay and you don't try to throw her out, she too will leave by herself, never to return. One by one, different things arrive in this room and, one by one, through non-attached awareness, we let them go.

If we let go a little, there is a little peace.
If we let go a lot, there is a lot of peace.
If we let go completely: complete peace.

The important thing to understand here is that we only ever let go of the conditions that take us into unhappiness.

Happiness is not something that we need to create in our life, for the natural state of the mind is to be happy. All we need to do is let go of the habits of mind that cover that intrinsic happiness.

The sun is always shining, even of we can't see it. We don't need to create the sun; we only need to wait for the clouds that obscure it to fall away. This is the practice of Insight meditation, known as Vipassana.

So now we can begin our practice: to sit for twenty minutes, our attention centred upon the touch sensation of breath and being aware, through the practice of Bare Attention, of the natural and unrestricted movements of mind.

Please take your posture and close your eyes…

Vipassana practice (part two)

Happiness is elusive, to say the least, and cannot be guaranteed by simply getting what you want. As you continue with your daily practice of Bare Attention, you will find that, naturally and spontaneously, your understanding deepens. Consistency is the key to this and it is always better to sit for a short time each day, rather than one very long meditation sit at the weekend. To assist with the spiritual understanding of this being that we call 'self', here is a short story from the Buddhist tradition.

The Buddha had a way of teaching that attracted people from all walks of life. From the lowest in the land to the highest, people would seek him out for instruction.
King Pasenadi of Kosala and his wife queen Malika were supporters and practicing disciples of the Buddha, even to the point of receiving meditation instruction from him. The land in that part of India was very beautiful but also very flat, so king Pasenadi ordered a magnificent tower to be built so that he and his queen could climb to the top and survey their kingdom. Often they would ride out with their entourage to enjoy the peace and quiet and to gaze out over the land they ruled.
On one of these occasions, whilst standing in silence at the top of the tower, both king Pasenadi and queen Malika shared the same intense meditation experience. They did not speak about it until they returned to the ground and were sitting astride their horses. The king asked his queen what had happened to her. She replied

that when she was standing silently and peacefully at the top of the tower, her mind calm and focused, she had experienced a profound insight into the real nature of her life. She realised, with complete intuitive understanding, that the person she loved most in the whole world was herself! This was incredible, for king Pasenadi had experienced the same intuitive understanding that the person he loved most in the world was himself. They had both realised that, even if they were married and loved each other and, even if they had children and many other relatives and friends around them, even if they had their favourite animals at the palace, the person they each loved the most, in every moment, was themselves. They saw that, on an obvious gross level and even on a more subtle and refined level, they always put themselves and their personal desires first. Having recounted this remarkable insight to each other, they rode to the camp of the Buddha to share their understanding with him.

"This is good", said the Buddha, after they had explained everything to him. "Now the spiritual life can truly begin."

Each one of us lives in a world created by ourselves. This world is established upon our habits of liking and disliking, of continually picking and choosing one thing over something else. In this world there is never any peace, because there is always something else to get.

We place ourselves and our desires at the very centre of this world and then demand that everyone and everything we meet always please and satisfy us. Just like King Pasenadi and Queen Malika, the person we each love most in this world is ourselves and we will do almost anything to produce those subtle and gross feelings called happiness that we crave so much. If we are not able to experience those feelings in any particular moment, we will blame everyone and everything outside ourselves for not being perfect and disappointing us.

Without realising it, we try to control the whole universe – insisting that everyone and everything always be the way we want them to be. We don't want it to rain on our picnic and become angry when it does. We expect our child to do well in school and become disappointed when they don't. We want our marriage to last forever and suffer the depths of disappointment when it collapses. We perform a kind action for someone and become upset when it isn't acknowledged with even a 'thank you'.

Without wisdom, this is how we meet our life. We place ourselves in the centre of our own universe, with very clear ideas of how everyone and everything should be all the time. Because we are always attempting to manipulate our happiness above the natural unfolding of events, always trying to make favourable things occur, whilst at the same time preventing unfavourable things from taking place, we are actually conditioning the arising of all our experiences of unhappiness. This unhappiness manifests as fear, disappointment, frustration, anger and the rest. It is an endless battle, attempting to control everything so that we can feel secure in life, so that we can be happy.

When we examine the feelings of happiness that we crave so much, we will see that they have their foundation in three types of ideas we carry, based in our own selfish motivation.

The first idea is to get something that we don't have, which we feel will make us happy. The new smart phone, tablet, car, home entertainment system, promotion at work, a new relationship… The list is endless, but is always preceded by the thought: "If only I had that, then I'd be happy."

We can spend many long years pursuing this idea of fulfilling our wish list to bring lasting happiness into our life, but the very moment we feel that we have arrived at the end of our list we will turn the page to see that it goes on forever. And this list is not only material things. Items such as looking for the perfect partner, the perfect job and the perfect life are also written on it. Even political, religious and social views and opinions are part of this list, established in the thought: "If only the world and everything in it was the way I want it to be, then I'd be happy."

Even when we find a formula that once resulted in the experience of happiness, it cannot be guaranteed to be successful a second time. The wonderful party on Friday evening may or may not be as wonderful the next week, even though it is with the same people, the same music and at the same location. Happiness is elusive, to say the least, and it cannot be guaranteed by simply getting what we want.

The second idea that we carry is that of pushing something away that we believe is making us unhappy. Again, the list of things that we attribute our unhappiness to is endless. An illness, the stress from work or family life, an old car that is no longer reliable, a difficult romantic relationship… We feel that: "If only I didn't have this, then I'd be happy."

However, we have to be careful here also, because we can spend our whole life pushing away the things that we feel are making us unhappy, only to find that there is always one more thing to get rid of. As long as we attribute our unhappiness to external conditions, we will always be able to blame other people and situations for how we feel.

The third idea that we carry with us, concerning our endless quest for happiness, is the notion that: "I'll do something now so that I'll be happy in the future." It is the idea that for the next ten years we will work hard and save our money so that we can retire early, find an island in the sun and open a beach bar – then we'll be happy! It is the delusion that this time now doesn't count for anything, except to prepare for the future.

It is not necessary to be enlightened to see the flaw in

this argument. Life is uncertain and we cannot truly say what will happen in the next ten minutes, never mind the next ten years. To base happiness on a vague notion sometime in an imaginary future is not very wise and, more that that, we miss what is happening right now.

All too often, happiness is perceived as a goal in the future: "I'm not happy now, but if I can just get all the things I want, and get rid of all the things I don't want, then I will be happy." Society is complicit in this delusion, of course, through the media and advertising, always promoting happiness in the future. When you have the right car, woman, man, perfume, etc, etc, you will be happy. Of course you are not enough now, but with all these necessary things that we can sell you, happiness awaits.

This is the great social manipulation: that whatever you aspire to be, it will never be enough.

The idea of doing something now, not for what we can experience now but for some goal in the future, is often the reason why people come to meditation practice. The feeling is something like: "I'll meditate now so that I will be enlightened (happy) in the future."

At the beginning, this way of thinking is accepted because we need to feel that meditation will actually lead us somewhere and that we will receive some benefit. As a goal orientated culture, it is hard to ignore this reasoning before better understanding arises.

A woman once came to me to learn meditation. When I asked her why she wanted to begin this beautiful practice, she replied: "Because I want to stop being angry in every situation." To me, this seems like a very good reason to begin.

However, with the understanding cultivated through our practice, we will realise directly and intuitively the true nature of mind and body and so live peacefully and harmoniously with them. We will bring ourselves to the present moment and let go of trying to determine happiness in the future.

The purpose of Anapanasati, for example, is to be with the sensation established in the nostrils as the body breathes. It is not to try and create special feelings of peace and calm. However, by quietly sitting with Anapanasati and without any ulterior motive, peace and calm naturally arises. As with all things, it is our attitude and intention that gives value to what we do.

At one time there was a young disciple who was very intent on his meditation practice. He would arrive in the meditation hall early in the morning before everyone else, he would stay later than everyone else and give his whole time to meditation.
One day the master noticed this young disciple alone in the meditation hall, entered and sat down quietly next to him.
"What are you doing", asked the master.
"I'm meditating to produce enlightenment", replied the

disciple.

On hearing this, the master stood up and left the meditation hall. He returned a few minutes later with a small stone he had taken from the garden. Sitting down next to the disciple, he began to rub the stone rhythmically on his robe.

Not able to ignore this strange behaviour, the disciple couldn't help but ask: "Master, what are you doing?"

The Master replied: "I am polishing this stone to produce a diamond."

The disciple was astonished. "How can polishing a stone produce a diamond?"

The Master answered: "How can sitting in meditation produce enlightenment?"

Our life is always about this moment, NOW. Everything that is not this moment is a fantasy, an imagination. The past is only a memory and a memory is only a thought.

And when do you experience this thought? Now, only ever now!

The future is only a mental projection and that mental projection is only a thought.

And when do you experience that thought? Now, only ever now!

In reality it is always now and can only ever be now.

It is now that you can do something; it is now that you can realise your own happiness, by letting go of the delusive conditions of mind that keep you searching outside this moment. Was I happier then…? Will I be happy in the future…?

Our attitude to practice and to life itself is the most important thing. To see reality as it actually is, moment after moment, and not be fooled by appearances, brings a joy and freedom that cannot be imagined before you experience it for yourself.

So, the teaching of Vipassana is: "Don't get lost in the mind". Everything is arising and passing away, according to its nature. None of it is yours, none of it is you and none of it is what you are. As this understanding becomes more firmly established, our quality of life increases, naturally and by itself.

Vipassana shows us the nature of the mind and of life itself and how to live peacefully in the world, surrounded by a myriad of things we cannot control. This, of course, not only includes, but actually begins with, our own mind and body.

The way to live peacefully in the world and experience real happiness is to let go of trying to control everyone and everything and simply be open to the infinite possibilities that life offers. It is to put down the limitations we place upon ourselves.

We have to allow everything to be just as it is and respond to each situation from wisdom, rather than from fear.

Conventionally, of course, we have to live in the world, which means that we have to make choices and decisions for ourselves and those we feel responsible for. Based in our growing understanding arising from our practice of Vipassana, however, we will know intuitively when to act and when to be still, when to speak and when to stay quiet, when to plan and when to simply let life take its own direction.

So, please assume your posture, close your eyes and continue with this beautiful practice of Vipassana, in the style of Bare Attention.

Vipassana

Week Three

Opening the heart
Metta Bhavana (Loving Kindness meditation)
For us to live with the things we like is not a problem.

With the development of Anapanasati, you are able to rest your attention on the touch sensation of breath at the nostrils. With the development of Vipassana you are able to experience the true nature of the mind and body, without reacting to whatever is presented to you.

Now comes the development of the third part of the practice, called Metta Bhavana in the Buddhist language of Pali, but more popularly known as Loving Kindness. It is this very important practice that brings harmony into our life as we let go, little by little, of the fear aspect of living. But, we first need to understand the use of the word 'love'.

In spiritual teaching, we can say that there are two kinds of love: that which is love and that which we call love. From the Vipassana perspective, what we call love – that we fall into and fall out of again, that which we write our songs, movies and plays about – is not love. It is only ever an attachment.

We love our parents because they are our parents. We

love our partner because they are our partner. We love our children because they are our children. We don't love all children! If we loved all children we would love everyone in the world, because everyone is someone's child.

Romantic or emotional love is only ever an attachment to something. Now, there is nothing wrong with that and the only thing we have to understand is that whatever we are attached to will hurt us. If it is our child that is sick, as parents we suffer. If it is our sports team that looses, we suffer. Suffering is always conditioned by attachment, whether to a person, material possession, spiritual, political or religious idea. Whatever we are attached to will hurt us.

This is important to understand. There is nothing wrong with attachment; it is a fun game to play, provided that we are able to accept the other side of it.

Spiritual love (Metta Bhavana) is a non-attached relationship to life and everything it contains. Whereas romantic love always comes with a list of conditions, Metta Bhavana makes no conditions about the quality of the relationship.

Romantic love often says: "You must be different (so that I can be happy)". Spiritual love says: "I accept you exactly as you are (because my happiness does not come from, nor depend on you)".

Spiritual love is the ability to be with things as they are, without demanding that they should be different in any way. And the question that you need to honestly reflect upon at this point is: why would you demand that something be different from the way it is?
The answer: so you can be happy, of course!

A female student of mine once telephoned me, to tell me that she had begun a new relationship with a man. "He's really lovely", she said, "I only have to change him a little."

Spiritual love can be defined as unconditional acceptance and is the true power in our life. For us to live with the things we like is not difficult. Puppy dogs and kittens, polite and well mannered people and wise spiritual teachers are easy, but ordinary life can bring many difficulties, being surrounded by the things that we don't like.

Arrogant people, noisy neighbours, mosquitoes and dogs that bark all night are some examples of these difficulties. These things can make our life seem intolerable and so we fight and argue, in order to make everything different – more suitable for ourselves. This battle never ends, until we change our whole perspective on life and begin to accept, lovingly, the way things are. This may imply simply giving up but, in actual fact, it means putting ourselves in a position of control.

It is here that we must understand that love is not liking

and that, in our practice of Metta Bhavana, we will not suddenly like all the things that actually we don't like. Liking and disliking are natural states of mind and if we don't like something, we don't like it – no need to pretend something else.

But even if we don't like it, we can still love it. We can still accept it without demands. It is from this position of unconditional acceptance that we can respond wisely in the world.

Reaction comes from fear (the antithesis of love) and the mind that screams: "It shouldn't be like this!" Response comes from love and the mind that says: "It is like this, now what do I really want to do with this situation?"

If we truly are the cause of our own unhappiness, then we can actually do something about it. We don't have to wait for our partner to be different before we can be happy; we don't have to wait for our children to be different before we can be happy; we don't have to wait for the world to be different before we can be happy. Happiness is right here, right now and all we have to do is reconnect with it.

Our experience of unhappiness beings and ends within our own mind, not outside it. The moment we change the way we usually view life and open our heart, with unconditional acceptance, our unhappiness falls away. By itself. We don't have to get rid of it, we only have to release our grip and it will fall away by itself. Metta Bhavana is releasing the grip on our unhappiness.

When we don't make demands on anything, it means that we are at peace with whatever is happening in that moment. Even if we don't want it, even if we don't like it, even if it is painful, we are accepting of the reality of the moment. This also means that the judgement and criticism of others falls away, naturally, and we understand the phrase:

Beings are the way they are; that is their choice.
But, you are the way you are and that is your choice.

The whole of our Dhamma practice can now be understood quite simply and profoundly, as follows:

With awareness we see.
With love we accept.
With wisdom we respond.

This is the whole of Dhamma.

The cultivation of loving kindness meditation allows us to see and then let go of our desire to control everyone and everything and let all beings be, just as they are. However, there is one important point to note, and this is crucial to complete understanding: that before we can have love (unconditional acceptance) for others, we must first have it for ourselves.

It is as though I invite you to my home for a meal. Before I can share this food with you, I have to have it for myself. Once I have it, I can share it with others.

This is the correct understanding of loving kindness.

Loving kindness means the cultivation of a heart that accepts without conditions and is all encompassing. It does not choose or select, but shares itself equally and with all beings. Friends and enemies alike become equal objects of this practice, as we live in peace more and more with beings exactly as they are.

We will understand that all cruel, unkind and selfish acts come from a mind not in harmony with itself and still under the influence of desires and aversions; and that the person continually empowering these qualities of mind must meet their consequence, sooner or later.

The potential for all human beings is a life established in love; a life where they will contribute something worthy to all their relationships and always be strong. The person manifesting loving kindness can never be the victim in any situation.

One student asked me: "If I have only love in my heart, won't others be able to take advantage of me?"
I could only reply that: "If others take advantage of you, it's because you don't have love in your heart."

The first person we have to love is ourselves. The moment we truly love ourselves, how can we allow others to abuse us? Love will not permit that, for ourselves or others. From the loving heart comes the falling away of judgement and criticism. This does not mean that we are unable to act in the world, but only that we stop manipulating others into predetermined categories for our own emotional and psychological security.

It is our wish within this practice that all beings, without exception, be well and happy, and this wish begins with ourselves. Loving kindness begins in our own heart: first for ourselves and then radiated outwards into the world and universe, to all living beings. Liking and disliking, approval and disapproval are not considerations. Liking and disliking is completely personal and based upon our old habits of mind. Love is universal and offered to all beings equally, whether we have some good feeling for them or not.

Metta Bhavana: the meditation

As you bring to an end your usual twenty minute session of Vipassana meditation, you will immediately begin your loving kindness practice. One develops into the other and there is no separation between the two.

First, we take our attention away from the breath and place it lightly on the top of the head. You will just notice if you are aware of any sensations, as you rest your attention there. It you feel something, good; if you feel nothing, good. In the whole of Vipassana practice, we are never trying to create a special event in the meditation. We are simply being with things as they are.

Now we gently pass the awareness down through the body, simply being aware of any sensations or impression the body might offer to us. This is not a long process and so should take only about one minute. When you have arrived at the soles of your feet, return your attention to the breath. This simple exercise establishes a 'sense of self': something that, at the beginning, we can direct our loving kindness towards and then, later, outwards from.

In this practice of loving kindness meditation you will wish yourself freedom from eight unwholesome states of mind – states of mind which, when empowered, take you only to unhappiness. Please note that we do not say that these mind states are wrong, wicked or evil, but merely unwholesome and so ultimately unhelpful for your happiness.

The eight unwholesome mind states are: anger, ill will, fear, anxiety, suffering, pain, ignorance and desire.

Then you will begin the cultivation of five wholesome states of mind. These are: happiness, peacefulness, harmony, liberation from greed, hatred and delusion and the realisation of the deeper peace within.

When you mentally recite this beautiful formula you must empower each phrase, giving it vitality and meaning. I'm sure it is quite possible to train a parrot to recite the loving kindness verse but, just because it can repeat the words, it does not mean that it understands the significance of them! If you want to change your heart, and so change your life, you must make the effort.

Loving Kindness Meditation (1)

May I be free from anger and ill will.
May I be free from fear and anxiety.
May I be free from suffering and pain.
May I be free from ignorance and desire.
May I be happy and peaceful.
May I be harmonious.
May I be liberated from greed, hatred and delusion.
May I realise the deeper peace within.

May all beings be free from anger and ill will.
May all beings be free from fear and anxiety.
May all beings be free from suffering and pain.
May all beings be free from ignorance and desire.
May all beings be happy and peaceful.
May all beings be harmonious.
May all beings be liberated from greed, hatred and delusion.
May all beings realise the deeper peace within.

It is important to understand that the eight unwholesome conditions of mind are old and familiar friends to us and, even if we want not to meet them again, they will still visit us from time to time. The teaching of loving kindness is not to annihilate these qualities when they appear in front of us, but with awareness to see them and with love to allow them to be there, without acting upon them. This way they will leave by themselves, gently and gradually over time (Visudhimagga).

So, now to begin the first part of the loving kindness practice with the phrase and wish: "May I be free from ..."

May I be free from anger...

Whenever anger is present in our mind, we become dangerous people. Even when we can justify and explain our anger, it never can bring a good result. In the state of anger we can hurt others with our actions and speech and our life experience will show us that often saying 'sorry' is too late.

The Buddha reminds us that, in the face of an enemy, we are already defeated when we display anger. Better to let go of the desire to strike out and remain in our loving centre of balance.

To be free from this unwholesome state of mind means to make our life more peaceful and harmonious, as well as not inflicting pain or discomfort onto others by our poor behaviour. Without the quality of anger in our life we will not suffer or, in the conventional sense, be the cause of suffering to others.

...and ill will.

Ill will means to have a bad feeling for another person and, like anger, is a manifestation of our own unhappiness. When you are angry, you are not happy; when you are happy, you are not angry. The two mind states cannot exist at the same time, in the same space.

Ill will means to resent the good fortune of others and often actually wish harm to another. There is no joy or lightness in this particular unwholesome state of mind and, if not released through the meditation practice of Vipassana, can actually condition illness in the body.

May I be free from fear...

Fear is the strongest factor in our lives. If happiness is our common human goal, fear is our common human experience. We are afraid of so many things that life ceases to be a joyful and exciting experience, but is rather seen to be a battle to control everything, so that we, and all the things we are attached to, can be safe.

We are afraid of ageing, dying, illness, separation, loss, being with things that we don't like, loosing things that we do like. So many reasons to be afraid, but, actually, we are just afraid of life itself!

The experience of fear is not a pleasant one, it is not something we ever seek and yet it is present so much of the time. It affects us mentally and physically and is the major obstacle to wisdom. The power of fear is immense and we don't have to be the one experiencing it to meet the effects of it. Everyone else's fear is manifesting it, to one degree or another.

Fear contracts the mind, limits our potential and inhibits

the generation of feelings of unconditional love. For all these reasons and more, it is a mind state that we wish ourselves freedom from.

…and anxiety.

Anxiety is similar to fear. It is an uncomfortable feeling in the mind and can be easily experienced in the body. Anyone who has had to wait to see the dentist or even the bank manager may well understand the feelings of anxiety. To sit with stomach churning, a dry mouth and sweaty palms is not a pleasant experience and leaves us a long way from peace. It well understood now that the long term physical effects of anxiety can lead to illness in the body and so freedom from it can only be beneficial, both mentally and physically.

May I be free from suffering…

Suffering here means mental distress, such as sorrow, grief, lamentation and other states of mind associated with loss or separation. To be free from the pain of these feelings will mean that we have understood and harmonised with the truth of all relationships: that whatever begins must end and that whatever comes together must separate.

Whether this ending is final, as in the death of a loved one, or temporary, as when we say goodbye at an airport or railway station, we will be able to peacefully be with these changing circumstances as they manifest as a natural part of life.

'May I be free from suffering' means to be balanced and at peace with the world, by no longer attempting to hold on to those things which, by their very nature, are already moving away from us.

Everything that is born must die. This is an unchanging truth and, no matter how unpleasant it may seem, each of us will one day have to meet the death of someone or something close to us. When we have understood the true nature of all relationships, we will be able to let them go peacefully and with compete acceptance. This is to truly be free from suffering.

...and pain.

Pain means physical pain. No-one enjoys painful conditions in the body, but we all have to endure them from time to time. Pain is inevitable in life, in the same way as old age, sickness and death. It is the nature of the body. To have a body means that we will always be subject to pain, for the natural disposition of the body is to be painful. Whichever position we place it in, whether in bed, in an armchair or just sitting on the floor, painful sensations will arise and we find ourselves changing posture to avoid them. However, this process is endless and we spend our life moving away from painful conditions only to find more waiting for us, usually not very far into the future.

'May I be free from pain' does not mean 'May pain

never arise in my body'. Rather, it means: 'May I understand the true nature of pain and so be released from the constant cycle of moving and stillness'. It is true to say that when wisdom arises, pain ceases.

May I be free from ignorance…

Ignorance is the basis for all unwise action. Ignorance simply means 'not to know' and if we don't know something, we just don't know. In this sense, we can say it is a blameless state. However, our usual life is established upon this sense of not knowing.

It is likened to living in a completely dark room. We have eyes and yet can't see anything. Inside this room are many other people, all in the same condition and, even though no-one can see anything, everyone is moving around and bumping into different pieces of furniture and each other, being hurt in the process. And when we are hurt, through moving around blindly in the dark, we always say the same thing to each other: 'It's your fault I'm hurt, you did this to me!'

This is the nature of ignorance. It is not a crime, it is not a sin, but it is the foundation of unhappiness.

…and desires.

Desire is the action arising from ignorance. It is desire that keeps us wandering around in this completely dark room, on our endless quest for happiness. When desire arises, we are able to perform any kind of harmful action or say anything to achieve our goal. Desire is always based in self interest and so when ignorance falls away, desire has nothing left to hold on to. The consequence is a flowing, harmonious and peaceful life, arising from the open and loving heart.

Perhaps you will wonder how it is possible to live without desire.

When ignorance falls away, desire has nothing left to hold on to; what remains are only our preferences in life. If someone offers you a choice of tea or coffee, you can easily choose the one you prefer. If, however, even having asked for tea, you are presented with coffee, you are still able to accept it graciously and enjoy it. This is because it was only a preference and not a desire. To drink coffee whilst wishing it was a nice cup to tea is just more suffering!

It is said that in the heart of the wise person there are no desires, only preferences. This is the way to live easily and comfortably in the world.

The five wholesome states

May I be happy…

It seems to be almost a spiritual secret, but the truth is that we are all entitled to be happy as much as anyone else – not more, but never less.
If this sounds selfish to you, please reflect for a moment.

When you are happy, you are a pleasure to be with. You are kind, generous and amusing. You are good company and you share the best qualities of yourself. Whatever mind state we experience, we share with the world – good or bad, happy or unhappy. It is the same for everyone.

Remember when you were a child and your mother was in a good mood? She would play with you, take you to the park and let you lick the mixing bowl when she was baking. When she was in bad mood, however, the best thing to do was to keep out of her way. Not only mothers are like this; it is the way of things. So, the best thing for you is to be happy and share that with the world.

However, from the perspective of loving kindness, happiness is not based on satisfying yet another self centred desire; rather, it is the opposite. Here happiness means losing self interest and being able to live life without continually seeking diversions and distractions to make it better. It means to celebrate life in an easy and wholesome way, taking delight in the simplest things and enjoying each moment as it comes.

...and peaceful.

Peacefulness is a true gift in our life: the ability to see things in perspective and to stop riding our emotional roller coaster. With a life established in wisdom we will respond to situations, rather than blindly reacting. Response comes from acceptance of the reality of the moment; reaction comes from fear, from the voice that shouts: "It shouldn't be like this!"

Everything in our life is always changing. Because of the loving space we now allow in our mind, we are able to see and understand things clearly. This space is peace.

It is true to say that some people experience situations that are problems, whilst other people experience problems that are just situations – something to simply respond to and pass through. Remembering that the world we experience is the one that we create for ourselves, moment after moment, we will be able to keep things in perspective and not overreact.

May I be harmonious.

Harmony is the key to loving kindness. To live peacefully amongst all the things that cause annoyance in the world is a very skilful thing to do. The secret to this is 'not to mind': that is, to accept the reality of the moment and then respond.

Through the practice of Vipassana and Metta Bhavana, we will cultivate a harmonious relationship with this mind and body, which produces a harmonious relationship with life.

It is our relationship to this mind and body that determines our relationship to life. From this position of harmony we will bring something of value to each situation, rather than simply adding to the confusion that already abounds in the world.

May I be liberated from greed, hatred and delusion.

These are the three fires that burn within us all and are the conditions of mind that manifest ignorance.

Greed displays itself as the desire to get something it doesn't already have, with the thought: 'If only I had that, then I'd be happy.'
Hatred displays itself as the desire to push away something it doesn't want, with the thought: 'If only I didn't have that, then I'd be happy.'

Delusion is the part of the mind that cannot see beyond this cycle of acquiring and rejecting and, so, controls our behaviour.

This, of course, is a very simple explanation of these three root causes of our cyclic life, but suffice to say that to no longer be a victim to them would be a very welcome thing indeed. This would be a real liberation from the true causes of our unhappiness.

May I realise the deeper peace within.

Each one of us lives on a very superficial level of mind: that of greed, hatred and delusion. It is this mind that will fight, argue and do whatever it can to control everyone and everything, so that life is always perfect for us. And, of course, it is this mind that can always justify and rationalise its behaviour.

The moment we learn to let go even a little of our attachment to this way of being, we will experience the deeper peace within. This peace, because it is not conditioned by the outside world, is called 'Pure Mind'. This aspect of mind has no ego or self identity attached to it and, consequently, no suffering. It is only ego that suffers. Ego, or self identity, is that part of us that continually identifies with the mind as being who and what we are, and so is always trying to create perfect conditions to live under.

The Pure Mind arises when ego falls away. It is not something newly created by us, but rests submerged under the pressure of self identity: under the thoughts of 'I', 'me', 'mine' and 'my', and the dualistic world of opposites that these thoughts create.

When Pure Mind is present, it can only spontaneously manifest in one of four ways: unconditional love or acceptance, unconditional compassion or oneness, sympathetic joy or sharing in the good fortune of others, and equanimity or complete balance in life.

Our purpose in practice is not to kill the ego, but to love it to death. If it is only ego that suffers, it follows that the less ego is present in our life, the less suffering there will be. Through the practices of Vipassana and Metta Bhavana we will stop feeding the ego and allow it to fall away, gently and gradually, and experience the beauty of a life directed by Pure Mind.

This, then, is the meditation practice of loving kindness, directed towards ourselves. Once this list has been completed, we can sit for a few moments and allow our attention to go to the body. How do we feel right now? What is the physical effect (if any) of such a beautiful and heart opening practice?

Now we must radiate these feelings outwards from our heart, from our centre into the world and the universe, touching all beings equally and without exception.
This time we begin with the phrase:

May all beings be free from...

We then continue at the same gentle pace, until the eight unwholesome and five wholesome aspects have been mentioned. Again, you will sit for a few moments and take your attention to the body. When you radiate feelings of loving kindness to all beings, how does this feel?

The final part of this practice comes when we reflect upon particular beings in our life and offer loving kindness towards them. These are beings that often we find ourselves in conflict with and so we mentally generate an image of them and (mentally) say: "May you be well and happy".

It is important to understand that we do not offer loving kindness to these particular beings in order to change them (this cannot be done), but we offer loving kindness to them to change our relationship with them. This means that we accept them as they are, and then respond to their behaviour appropriately.

The list of people to reflect upon is as follows: our parents, spiritual teachers, immediate family, friends, relatives and acquaintances and, finally, someone that we don't like or have some difficulty with.
When we have finished this list, we can sit once again for a few moments and feel the effects of such a practice in the body. This long form of loving kindness meditation should last for approximately ten to twelve minutes, so your sitting time should now be half an hour.

If, on certain occasions, you do not have sufficient time for a thirty minute sit, you can use a short form of loving kindness. Simply repeat three or four times:

May I be well and happy,
may all beings be well and happy.

As always, we must remember to put energy into our practice to make it something vibrant and alive.

One final version of loving kindness practice has the emphasis on acceptance. This is as follows:

May I accept other beings
exactly as they are in this moment.
May I accept this moment exactly as it is.
May I accept myself exactly as I am in this moment.

Repeat three times.

Loving Kindness Meditation (2)

May I be free from anger and ill will.
May I be free from fear and anxiety.
May I be free from suffering and pain.
May I be free from ignorance and desire.
May I be happy and peaceful.
May I be harmonious.
May I be liberated from greed, hatred and delusion.
May I realise the deeper peace within.

May all beings be free from anger and ill will.
May all beings be free from fear and anxiety.
May all beings be free from suffering and pain.
May all beings be free from ignorance and desire.
May all beings be happy and peaceful.
May all beings be harmonious.
May all beings be liberated from greed, hatred and delusion.
May all beings realise the deeper peace within.

Now to offer love and acceptance to: your parents, your spiritual teacher, your immediate family, your friends, relatives and acquaintances and, finally, someone that you don't like or are having some difficulty with.

The essence of this beautiful teaching of love, compassion and unconditional acceptance is expressed in this simple verse taken from the Buddhist Metta Sutta:

May all beings be happy and secure, may their hearts be wholesome.
Whatever living beings there may be, feeble or strong, tall, stout or medium, long, short or small, seen or unseen, those living far or near, those who are born and those who are to be born, may all beings, without exception, be happy.

To radiate these thoughts to the world and universe will bring happiness and peace into the life of the practitioner and bring benefit to all beings.
This is the value of Loving Kindness practice.

Please assume your posture, close your eyes and begin your daily meditation, ending with the loving kindness practice.

Vipassana

Week Four

Awareness in daily life
The effects of the world are very strong.

Through the practice of Vipassana, in the form of Bare Attention, we have been able to experience directly the real nature of mind and body. That the mind is a constant stream of thoughts, moods, feelings and emotions and that the body is the object of pleasure and pain. With this simple investigation, we can know for ourselves exactly where all the difficulties of life we encounter really begin. Not outside, with other people and events, but here in the mind-body complex.

As one teacher said: "There are no problems in the world, you are the problem!"

With the insights and understanding gained, we can now see the danger in allowing all the attachments, wrong views and misunderstandings that we carry with us to go unchallenged.

The ensuing result of Vipassana meditation is a growing sense of freedom in life, as we simply learn to let go of all the different conditions that lead us only ever towards unhappiness. Our life becomes purer as the motivation for our actions becomes clearer. Perhaps you have already begun to experience the beautiful results of this essentially simple practice?

The third part of your daily meditation is the loving kindness: the way of living in harmony with the world and all beings. From this part of your practice, you will have begun to build your capacity for unconditional love, compassion and respect for all the beings that we share the planet with and the space to allow them to be exactly as they are.

You may not personally like or approve of their life style or habits but with your developing heart these things will trouble you less and less. With wisdom you will know when to act and when to be still, when to speak and when to be silent.

Your daily sitting practice should now last for about thirty minutes, although you can easily extend this time if you are comfortable with that. On retreats and courses, the usual sitting time is forty-five minutes.

Sitting more than once a day can also be developed, for example morning and evening time, but family considerations must be taken into account. This meditation practice must serve to enhance our life and the lives of those around us. It is not to cause further confusion and divisions by callously excluding family and friends. However, personal circumstances apart, it is important to give your meditation time each day a much higher priority than watching television or dozing in the armchair after work.

In this final part of the course we look at how to take our experiences and understanding cultivated through practice into daily life.

The central part of our practice is devoted to gaining clear insight into the nature of our existence. This is achieved by calmly and dispassionately observing, or more accurately experiencing, the natural dispositions of mind and body. Because there is no practice outside ourselves (we only ever observe our reactions to the event of the moment and not the event itself), there is not time when this practice cannot be applied.

It should be understood that our meditation practice must have more value than simply sitting quietly once or twice a day and coming away from that with a good feeling. There are many meditation practices like this and they are good as far as they go, but soon the pleasant feeling coming from the meditation falls away and we are left living in the world, facing the same problems and difficulties and still chasing those elusive feelings of happiness. In this situation, meditation can be seen as a temporary escape from the world, rather than a meeting of the world – our world, the one that we create and maintain through the habits of mind.

Consider a garden lawn. If a weed grows in the middle of the lawn, it is not enough to merely pass the lawnmower over it occasionally and leave it at that. It is true that for a short time the weed cannot be seen and so the whole garden looks beautiful, but soon it shows itself once more and has to be cut back again. The only way to free the garden from this weed is to remove it from the roots. This way it cannot grow back.

This is the function of Vipassana meditation: to eradicate the very causes of our experience of unhappiness, instead of merely addressing the symptoms of it. After all, this is what we have been doing for all of our lives, addressing only the manifestation of our unhappiness and not the true cause. It is this unsatisfactory experience of life that has led you to this course of Vipassana and Metta Bhavana practice.

Only two things are required for this unique form of meditation. We don't need to create a special shrine or become involved in a new and exotic religion, as tempting as that is for many people. We don't need to wear a spiritual uniform or style our hair in a special way to show we belong to a particular group. We don't even need to sit in a special posture.

The only requirements for practice and, ultimately, complete awakening are mind and body, and these are the two things we always have with us.

It is not possible to say: "I'm sorry but I can't meditate today, I didn't bring my mind with me"! Everything we need for practice is with us at all times, therefore the opportunity for practice is with us at all times. The rest is up to us.

Do you see this as a moment to practice or not? Do

you recognise that this moment, no matter how uncomfortable it may seem right now, is the perfect moment to apply awareness to see, love to accept and wisdom to respond?

Traditionally it is understood that there are only four postures the body can assume, although there are obvious variations on these. The point is that no matter what posture the body takes, awareness and loving kindness can always be established.

Sitting

The sitting posture obviously includes our formal meditation position, however that is. As that will have been well established by now, nothing more need be said about it. However, by deliberately restricting the movements in the body we are able to see the natural flowing of the mind. We can experience through our physical posture how the mind struggles to be free from its containment and so our desire to move, to change posture for no real reason can sometimes be almost overwhelming. Although movement is not forbidden, it is discouraged in order to aid and assist determination and resolution in practice.

Outside formal meditation sessions there are obviously many times each day when we are sitting, whether we are at home, at work or even travelling by bus or train. We simply have to be aware of the physical posture and allow our awareness to pass through it, just noticing how it feels. Relax and centre ourselves, come back to a point of awareness. It does not need to be said that we should not do this whilst in the act of driving a vehicle, but only when we are travelling as a passenger.

With awareness we can experience the sensation of bodily contact with the seat and the floor, the feelings of comfort or discomfort that arise from this contact and, more importantly, our reaction to them.

Without awareness we can spend enormous amounts of time never sitting still, but always fidgeting and changing our position – always seeking the perfect posture that will not result in an uncomfortable sensation. However, with the cultivation of awareness we will notice dispassionately the different sensations in the body and so break our habit of simply reacting, by moving every time they appear.

We can apply awareness to the sitting posture even momentarily, for example, whilst watching television or waiting at the table for a meal to be served. Whenever we have a moment in the sitting posture we can apply awareness, by lightly giving our attention to the body or the touch sensation of breath in the nostrils. We can then return to whatever activity we were engaged in from a new position of spiritual or mental balance.

One small teaching from my own master, many years ago, was: "Whenever you are not doing something in

particular, meditate."
This does not mean to assume the formal posture, but to simply bring the awareness to the mind and body as they are in this moment, refreshing our awareness and energy and not being confused by the world around us.

Standing

Although there is a formal standing meditation posture, there is no need to explain it here. This posture would only ever be used on intensive Vipassana meditation retreats and then only after long hours of sitting practice. However, awareness applied to the body or breath whilst in the standing posture is a practice that can be used many times a day in ordinary life.

Once again, by directing our attention down through the body, relaxing our posture and patiently noticing the sensations, whether gross or subtle, coarse or refined, we can break our well established habits of simply moving away from anything we feel is uncomfortable. In this atmosphere of calm and peacefulness, we are also able to be with the mind as it moves – habitually picking and choosing, blaming and criticising, judging and commenting and never at peace. This is an excellent way to train, when we might be waiting in line for a bus or train or even at the supermarket checkout.

Walking

Walking meditation is a traditional practice dating back to the Buddha himself. It can be found in almost all of the Vipassana styles practiced today – usually on intensive retreats, where the programme will be a daily rhythm of sitting and walking practice.

The simple explanation behind walking meditation is that because we do not spend all our time sitting still, it is good to cultivate awareness of the body as it moves. This understanding then accompanies us into our daily life. So, outside of the retreat environment, awareness whilst walking can be applied wherever we are, such as at home, in the street, in the office or factory.

We begin by placing our awareness on the soles of our feet and walking to wherever we want to go in a relaxed but ordinary manner. We don't look at our feet, but merely become aware of the shifting sensations on the soles, as our body weight is applied and released with each step. This awareness can then be extended to include the whole body, simply noticing the movements of the ankles, knees, hips and torso, not forgetting the arms as they are lightly held in front of you or are relaxed by your side.

If we are in a more public place it is better etiquette to keep our practice of awareness whist walking as discreet as possible – not making a show of what we do, but making this training only for ourselves. Naturally, when practicing walking meditation, we need to cultivate a complimentary awareness of our surroundings, so that we are not bumping into others or, worse, stepping off the pavement into the path of oncoming traffic.

A slightly more advanced form of this practice is to silently offer loving kindness as we move, simply mentally repeating the formula:

> *May I be well and happy,*
> *may all beings be well and happy.*

Lying down

For most of us, lying down will mean being in bed. Each evening, before we go to sleep, and each morning, upon awakening, we have the opportunity to be aware. We can begin and end each day by centring ourselves and establishing balance.

Once we have assumed our preferred sleeping position we can pass the awareness lightly through the body and, as always, simply be aware of any sensations or impressions that the body may offer to us. We can also notice the weight of the bed clothes resting on us, the softness or firmness of the mattress and the sensation of comfort and warmth. Having done this we can give our attention to the breath and either begin or end our day with it.

If a time arrives when, for whatever reason, we cannot

fall asleep, this presents itself as an unexpected opportunity to practice awareness and loving kindness. We cannot force ourselves to fall asleep; we can only surrender into the tiredness, so relax, be with things as they are and let the breath come and go.

Summary

These four activities constitute daily practice outside our formal sitting time. As always, the primary object for cultivating awareness is the touch sensation of breath. Because this is a naturally occurring phenomenon, it can be contacted at any time, in any situation. This is why it is considered such a valuable gift in our life. In any moment we can find the sensation and re-establish focus, clear seeing and acceptance.

One aspect of daily life that affects many people is that of irritation or annoyance, caused by interruptions to our work, whether at home or in our employment. The conditions that give rise to these particular feelings are, of course, based in our own selfish desire for situations to always meet our idea of perfection. They are not founded in the wisdom of 'flowing with life'. Consequently we suffer, by giving away our power to conditions that we cannot control. The perfect attitude for our continued development is contained in the following verse:

In sitting, just sit.
In walking, just walk.
Above all, don't wobble!

Wobbling is the problem and it comes when we are trying to do more than one thing in any one moment.

As our practice of Anapanasati has shown us, when we are with the breath, we are not with thinking. When we are thinking, we are not with the breath.

The mind can only ever be in one place in any moment; in this place there is the peace and power called 'focused mind'.

Once we have learned to be with the one thing that we are doing in any particular moment, life will be much simpler and happier for us. No more will we walk into the path of an oncoming car, cut our finger with the bread knife or trip on our way down the stairs. With moment to moment awareness, we will give our flowing attention to each thing as it arises and so always be in control of the situation.

With this attitude of flowing awareness as the basis for everyday life, interruptions and distractions are never a problem. When our attention is required elsewhere, we can completely turn away from the task we are involved in and give our full attention to the new one. When that moment has passed we can return to the original task without the feeling of interruption, as our attention is simply moving from one impersonal thing to the next, according to the ever changing conditions of life.

To live a life without tutting and sighing each time we

are approached makes our presence much easier and joyful to be with. To have the time, patience and ability to be with the person you are supposed to be with is to bring a great gift to the world.

However, the effects of the world are very strong. People and situations will always attempt to take us away from our practice of love and awareness. The only way to counteract this influence from the world is to maintain our balance. Once we are established in our centre of peace and harmony, nothing can touch us. We are beyond the way of the world.

This is called: 'living in the world, but not being a part of the world'.

So, at the end of our course we can see that our potential for liberation is infinite; all we have to do is wake up in our life.

When we are dreaming, the dream that we are experiencing is real for us. If someone is chasing us with a gun or a knife in our dream, in that moment we experience all the fear attached to that situation. It is only when we wake up, we can breathe a sigh of relief and say: "Thank heavens, it was only a dream."

This is also the nature of our relationship with life, until we experience for ourselves, directly and experientially, the driving forces that continually move us in the same direction.

It is only Vipassana practice that will reveal these things to us and then only unconditional acceptance of them that will take away their power, until all that is left is the beautiful purity of being.

This is the gift that you give to yourself: a life without conditions, without demands, but simply responding – moment to moment.

This is the beauty and power of Loving Awareness.

May all beings be happy.

Questions and Answers

Question

By developing these meditation practices, will I loose my ambition or desire to succeed in business?

Answer

It seems to be true that only two kinds of people go into business: those who want to help others and those who want to help themselves. If your intention in business is to give a service that will benefit your customers or clients, and therefore yourself, then Vipassana and Metta Bhavana practice will certainly help you. Your attitude will become more and more one of endeavouring to serve the people who come to you and less of simply trying to undercut your competitor. Your motivation will become clearer and you yourself will become happier.

If your intention, however, is to get rich quick at any cost, this practice will not help at all. Vipassana practice is about being aware of the natural tendencies of the mind towards greed, hatred and delusion. As these movements become better known and better understood by us, the desire to act upon them falls away. We see them, we know them and we respond accordingly. The result of this is less greed, less hatred, less delusion and an understanding that everything we empower has a consequence for us. As we cannot avoid the consequence of what we do, it is always better to act from good intentions and clear motivation. This way we will be happy and share that happiness with the world.

Question

You mentioned 'Pure Mind'. Is it really feasible to develop a mind free from ego?

Answer

Pure Mind is not only feasible, but something that we actually experience many times a day. To perform an unselfish act spontaneously, without any thought of receiving something in return, is Pure Mind.

For example, an old lady in the street in front of you trips and falls heavily onto the pavement. Immediately you rush to her side to help, making sure that she is not hurt too badly. At her side you are filled with genuine concern for her well being, offering to take her to her home in your car or at least stay with her until a friend or a relative arrives. When someone does come they are full of gratitude for your kindness, but you, from the perspective of Pure Mind, walk away genuinely thinking: "But I didn't do anything." That is how Pure Mind manifests.

If, however, you saw the old lady trip and fall in the street and then looked around to see if anyone was watching your response to the situation (if you stopped to help, how much would it inconvenience you or how much it would improve your reputation amongst your friends and acquaintances?), that cannot be called Pure Mind. There is a clear agenda behind your response.

This is how the ego mind manifests in every situation, always asking: "What's in this for me?"

Spontaneity cannot be practiced or rehearsed. By definition it has to occur naturally, without any preconceived ideas. To empower the quality of Pure Mind means to cultivate the space where it can manifest. This is achieved by allowing all the different manifestations of ego to fall away. Not trying to destroy them or eradicate them violently, but gently, lovingly and patiently recognising the self oriented impulses and releasing them from our life.

We can reflect upon the Buddhist maxim, 'Never hesitate to do good', and use it as an inspiration in all our relationships.

This means not to miss an opportunity to help and serve other beings in the world – not only humans, but all beings that we came into contact with. This will greatly serve us in our ongoing spiritual development. However, we should always act immediately, for in that moment of hesitation all the selfish reasons to do nothing arise and then for us perhaps the moment is missed.

Actually, like all Dhamma teachings, it is very simple. If we can help we should help. If we can't help – don't interfere. Don't try to be anything, don't try to become someone or something; just be with the mind, as it arises and passes away, and let go of your attachment to what you meet as being who and what you are. When nothing is left in any moment there is Pure Mind.

Question
I have a lot of trouble with thoughts and emotions during meditation. What can I do about them?

Answer
When I trained in the Zen system of mediation we were taught, as an exercise, to sit in the posture that we first assumed. We had to bow to our zafu (meditation cushion), spin around on our heels and literally drop into our sitting posture. It had to be right first time, as we were not allowed to correct it later.

As foolish as this may sound, it was actually a very good training to develop the accepting mind – the mind that is not always preoccupied with choice. To accept our posture, without fidgeting, meant that we immediately had to give up our preferences towards physical comfort and, having done that, we could apply ourselves to the task in hand: that of observing the mind as it presented itself, moment after moment.

As human beings we have a natural inclination towards happiness, pleasure and comfort. These things always take a high priority in the way we organise our life. However, in Vipassana training, we actually observe the mind's own tendency towards choosing, but in that observation give up choice itself. To simply be with the contents of the mind as they appear, moment after moment, without complaining, comparing or wishing they were different, is the true practice of Vipassana. Like clouds that pass through an empty sky… Not me, not mine, not what I am.

So relax, there is no problem here – only mind moving. Once we develop an idea of how we want our meditation to be, we are always a long way from peace.

The secret to harmony in meditation and in life is not to mind. To accept what is presented to you in any moment and then respond. To do whatever is necessary.

Question
I like to wash the dishes whilst listening to the radio. Is this wrong?

Answer
To turn a mundane activity such as washing the dishes into a mindfulness experience can be a very rewarding thing to do. To notice one thing after another – the physical posture, the weight of the body as it stands at the sink, the feel of the water and its temperature, the dishes and the movement of your hands as you clean them – is excellent training. So many moments of awareness arising and passing away. In this activity, as with any other that we give our full attention to, full awakening can happen.

However, it is not necessary to do this every time you wash the dishes. Sometimes we can wash the dishes with full awareness and so develop the Vipassana practice. At other times we can wash the dishes with partial awareness, enjoying the activity and listening to the music or conversation on the radio.

Spiritual training should have the effect of making our life happier, to be able to enjoy that which can be enjoyed, and be open and accepting to those more difficult things that must be endured. There is no need to become so serious that everything becomes a drudge.

Question
You mention the Buddha often. Are you teaching Buddhism?

Answer
The simple answer is no. In fact, I am not teaching anything at all; I am simply sharing something with you. Although what we call Vipassana has come from the Buddha, it is not 'Buddhist'. Awareness and love cannot belong to any one group or organisation. They are spontaneous aspects of mind that already belong to everyone. However, we can explain and share the understanding of it so that others can apply these practices to their own life, to see if it has value or not.

I am never trying to convince or persuade you that I am right and that you must follow my way or, worse, accept my words without investigation. My purpose in front of you is to share Dhamma.

Dhamma is a Buddhist word that means something like 'the reality of things' or 'that which is behind the appearance of what is presented'. The tool used to see and experience the reality of things is awareness. Not more than that.

What is presented here is always testable in your own life. If you let go a little, is there really a little more peace in your life? You can know this directly, through your own practice, and you don't have to believe me or die to see if it is true. So, at best, I only encourage you to engage in this practice so that you will be happy and then share that happiness with all beings.

Question
For how long should I practice each day?

Answer
It is a common misunderstanding when people first begin to meditate that practice is one thing and ordinary life another.

This misunderstanding tends to be encouraged at the beginning, because of the way we are taught to meditate. We are told to find a suitable location – somewhere quiet and draught free, where we won't easily be disturbed – and to choose a time of day when the house is quiet and our family responsibilities are finished. These instructions encourage the idea that what we do is special and outside ordinary life. We do this at the start of Vipassana practice to not only support the necessary focus of mind and consequent awareness, but also to develop the habit of practice.

When we want to meditate, we should meditate. When we don't want to meditate, we should meditate anyway.

Once this habit of daily sitting is established, we can extend the non-attached relationship to the mind and its contents into every aspect of life, whether sitting, standing, walking or lying down. As always, the instruction is simple: quietly be aware of the natural movements of mind. Don't get lost in them, but recognise them for what they are. Bring yourself back to your centre – your point of balance – and move to the next thing.

Question
I want to say how pleased I am with this practice. Recently I found myself locked out of my house and I was really pleased with the way I handled the situation – much better, I'm sure, than I would have done a few weeks ago! Now I feel inspired to tell everyone about my Vipassana practice.

Answer
I am also pleased that you are experiencing good results from your practice; your desire to share what you have found is natural. For all of us, I think, when we discover something that makes us happy, we want to share it with others.

When I first became involved in Zen practice many years ago, I had a similar experience. I was very pleased with my apparent progress and would read everything I could about Zen and looked for every opportunity to discuss it with anyone who would listen. When I told my teacher about my wish to share all the wonderful things I had discovered through this practice, he very much supported me and even encouraged me to tell as many people as possible about the benefits of Zen training and all the good it could do in their lives, if only they would practice. I was elated. I felt like a missionary taking the good word out to the people.

I began straight away telling my friends, family and work colleagues as much as I could fit in to any conversation about Zen and its benefits. I quickly noticed, however, that no matter how enthusiastic I was, my words were not particularly well received and, more than that (perhaps it was my imagination), but people seemed to be actively avoiding me!

One day, whilst sitting having my lunch with a big rough and tough Welsh work colleague, I pointed to a tree and said: "Do you realise that it is the nothingness that surrounds the tree that gives it its shape?" Very deep! His verbal response I cannot give here, but suffice to say he was not impressed by my Zen observation.

It was at this point that I understood the teaching offered by my teacher. That is, when people want spiritual teaching they will ask for or move towards it themselves. It is unnecessary and often painful for us try to guide others towards it. If we are asked about what we are doing, we can answer clearly and from the heart – in a simple way that others can understand. If we want to have an effect on the world that we live in, let us do so from our example of wisdom, manifesting as love and compassion.

To want to share what we have discovered is a natural and beautiful thing. To make ourselves available to others, to help and give service is the best way to demonstrate this noble desire.

Question
How can I stop my mind from wandering?

Answer
The point here is not how to stop the mind from wandering, but only to know where it has wandered to. In the system of meditation known as Samatha Bhavana, a deep state of concentration is achieved by a concerted effort to keep the mind focused upon a single object. All other mental objects such as thoughts, moods,

feelings and emotions are considered to be hindrances and are excluded from a very narrow and precise field of awareness. The result, after many hours of practice, is a deep state of concentration (jhana), where normal mental faculties are suspended. This style of meditation, as a path to full spiritual understanding, was tried and tested and taken to its furthest extreme by the Buddha, before rejecting it for the practice we now call Vipassana.

We practice this form of meditation not to create any special kind of feeling or deep mental state, but to see the mind and body as they are in that moment. Even the aim, common in many new meditators, to sit in order to achieve a state of peacefulness and calm, is self defeating – by that very intention to create a particular mind state.

In Bare Attention practice, the primary object of awareness is the touch sensation of breath in the nostrils. However, the moment that another mental or physical activity occurs we should immediately let our attention go to that, before returning to the touch sensation of breath again. In this way everything that arises into consciousness becomes our meditation object, so, in real terms, it is not possible for the mind to wander at all. Not to be attached to thoughts, moods, feelings and emotions, as well as the sensations that arise in the body, will truly set us free. To be with things as they are is the way to realise this truth.

Question

Sometimes I just want to do more and more practice, but there are always so many obstacles in the way. What can I do?

Answer

Once, when I was staying at McCloud Gange in northern India, I climbed to the top of a waterfall. I was in the habit of taking an early morning walk after my meditation and had seen the waterfall from the road, so one day I took the decision to climb to the top.

After some time, the tarmac road gave way to a dirt road and, soon after that, no road at all! I was on the bed of the river, climbing over rocks and boulders, but always keeping the waterfall in front of me. The path now became steeper and more difficult, but with determination and effort I continued until I at last reached the top. However, as I took my last steps, sweating and breathing heavily, I saw to my amazement a cafe full of westerners drinking espresso coffee and listening to Bob Marley and the Wailers! They came up the easy way.

This can be likened to our practice. We can make it hard or easy for ourselves.

Hard means always attempting to create the right conditions for ourselves: the right room, the right silence, the right privacy, far away from the many distractions that prevent understanding form arising. The list of things that we need to be right for our practice, like all our lists in life, can be endless and as long as we continue trying to create perfect conditions for meditation, we will always be a long way from peace.

The easy way to practice is to recognise that the only things needed to develop that practice are always with us. It is our own mind and body, as they are in that moment; everything else is actually irrelevant.

So, when we feel that we can't practice because our mother-in-law arrives at the house just at the wrong time, the children are misbehaving and the dog is being sick on the carpet, just look at that. Look at the feelings and thoughts that arise within you. Don't react! No need to change anything – just be aware, then respond. Do whatever is appropriate to do. This is the way to train ourselves. This is the easy way.

To establish a practice based on a formal meditation sit each day is the best training, but we must be open to the changing conditions of daily life and be flexible. The teaching is around us all the time and in all places. It is not kept hidden in a secret location, known to only a few.

People used to go to India or Nepal to find themselves, but you only need to go to your meditation cushion. The necessary practice is always the same: be with the moment and respond. This is our practice.

Question

Do I need to live a moral life style?

Answer

What we actually experience in Vipassana meditation is the mental result of what we have empowered in the past. These memories and feelings arise in the mind when the usual activity of endless distraction is stopped – where they then have the space to become fully conscious.

We can say that 'evil' or 'wicked' people have a difficult time if left entirely to themselves, unless they keep their mind occupied even with such mundane activities as drinking and smoking. Once the external stimulus ends and the mind is left to itself, 'POP': up comes all the negativity and unwholesome mental states, and so further suppression is required not to meet them. Unless unwholesome intentions cease, this process of accumulation and suppression goes on and on, without end.

Of course, using words like 'evil' and 'wicked' implies only a very small number of human beings; mostly we do not think of ourselves in that way. However, it is hard to find someone who lives a perfectly pure life and, for all of us, our meditation is filled with the mental consequences of self identity and what we have empowered at different times. If not understood in the correct way, this self identity will compel us always to live our life at the centre of our own universe, where will demand that everyone and everything be the way we want them to be, so that we can be happy.

When the things we meet fail our demands to constantly please us, which of course they do, we can make many changes to ensure they fulfil our specific requirements! Depending on our natural tendencies, we can take bold steps indeed – often to the point of harming or even killing other beings, stealing, sexual misconduct, using our speech in cruel and harmful ways and using alcohol or drugs to alter the naturally occurring states of mind. To behave in this way is usually understood as 'immoral' behaviour.

Once we begin our path of spiritual awakening, we must be determined and resolute to change how we live. After all, changing your life is mostly about remembering to be different.

This is important to understand. We do not change our behaviour to appease a god or Buddha; we change our behaviour because both inside and outside of our meditation practice we will always meet the consequence of the mind that we have empowered. It is inescapable. And so, to be free from the endless procession of unsatisfactory and uncomfortable results, we must let go of the initial causes.

What we do, we do always for ourselves. So, we aspire to live a pure life – letting go of the lower and self-oriented aspects of mind, so that our lives become a blessing to us; but, more than that, a blessing to all the beings we share this planet with.

Question
Do we need to have contact with the teacher?

Answer
Although everything that needs to be done we have to do for ourselves, contact with someone who has walked the path before us is very important – someone with clear understanding and absolute integrity, who will support our practice and, equally as important, keep us facing in the right direction.

When I was teaching in India one time, a student asked me how she could know a good teacher. I could only answer: "Watch them when they are not teaching!"

We have to take care with those who proclaim spirituality, Dhamma and truth. The simple rule is: do they practice what they present and do they ask anything from you. Anyone can dress in a special style and offer themselves as a guru, smiling in a secret way, speaking in a hushed voice and creating the idea that they are different from you, but the true master lives with humility and integrity and sees their life only as service to the student.

Distraction and diversions are everywhere and, without a firm and secure foundation of practice, it is easy to become lost and wander off the path. The true master or teacher is our firm foundation.

The Tao Te Ching, the ancient Chinese book of wisdom, reminds us that: 'The path is straight, but people love to be sidetracked.'

It is true that often we can feel alone and isolated in our practice, although now, with the advent of modern technology, there is no real need to feel this way. Internet, CDs, DVDs and internet downloads, as well as email and Skype contact, can bring the Dhamma into our home whenever we need a reminder. Also, as teachers travel so much these days it is not too difficult to find a course, seminar or retreat close enough to you. It is no longer necessary to travel to India to find true meditation!

So, practice is everything and when our attitude is correct we can expect good results, but contact with an honest and reliable teacher is an enormous part of that.

May all beings be happy.

Acknowledgements

No book ever writes itself, and although the idea always seems simple, the actual work of sharing ones thoughts in a coherent way demands the help of others.

In this respect I feel blessed to have been aided by the people listed below, for their help, support and expertise.

Paul Quayle, for his support, advice and final proof reading of this version.

Isabelle Kewley, my wife, supporter and friend, who typeset the words and made them into the book you are holding.

To all my students and disciples for their encouragement to continually make the Pure Dhamma available so that all beings may benefit.

To these people and others I have not mentioned, I am as always, extremely grateful.

May they all be well and happy

About the author

Michael Kewley is the former Buddhist monk Paññadipa, who is now an internationally acclaimed Master of Dhamma, presenting courses and meditation retreats throughout the world. For many years he was the guiding teacher at the International Meditation Centre, Budh Gaya, India and is the founder of the Pure Dhamma tradition of spiritual awakening and the Being Awake meditation group network.

A disciple of the late Sayadaw Rewata Dhamma, he teaches solely on the instruction of his own Master; to share the Dhamma, in the spirit of the Buddha, so that all beings might benefit. On 26th May 2002, during a special ceremony at the Dhamma Talaka Temple in England, he was awarded the title of Dhammachariya.

A full biography of Michael Kewley, including videos and Dhamma talk extracts, can be found at:

www.puredhamma.org

Also by Michael Kewley

Higher than Happiness
Not This
Life Changing Magic
Walking the Path
The Other Shore
Life is not Personal
The Reality of Kamma
Buttons in the Dana Box
The Dhammapada

Lightning Source UK Ltd.
Milton Keynes UK
UKOW03f2252040913

216517UK00001B/2/P